44 Animals of the Bible

Written by **Nancy Pelander Johnson** | Illustrated by **Lloyd R. Hight**

First printing: September 2014

Master Books® is a division of the New Leaf Publishing Group, Inc.

ISBN: 978-0-89051-843-4
Library of Congress Number: 97-073934

Unless otherwise noted, Scripture quotations are from the New King James Version of the Bible.

Please consider requesting that a copy of this volume be purchased by your local library system.

Printed in China

Please visit our website for other great titles:
www.masterbooks.net

For information regarding author interviews, please contact the publicity department at (870) 438-5288

Master Books®
A Division of New Leaf Publishing Group
www.masterbooks.net

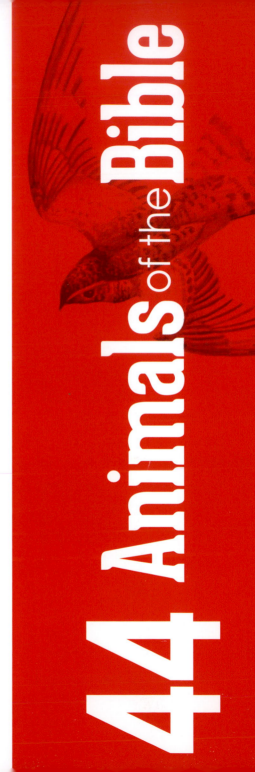

44 Animals of the Bible

1	ANT	23	MOLE
2	ASP	24	MOUSE
3	BADGER	25	NIGHTHAWK
4	CHAMELEON	26	OSPREY
5	DEER	27	OSTRICH
6	DOVE	28	OWL
7	EAGLE	29	PALMERWORM
8	FLY	30	PEACOCK
9	FOX	31	PELICAN
10	FROG	32	PYGARG
11	GIER	33	QUAIL
12	GOAT	34	RAM
13	HARE	35	SCORPION
14	HAWK	36	SPARROW
15	HERON	37	SWALLOW
16	HORSE	38	TURTLEDOVE
17	HYENA	39	TORTOISE
18	IBEX	40	UNICORN
19	KITE	41	VIPER
20	LAMB	42	VULTURE
21	LEOPARD	43	WEASEL
22	LIZARD	44	WHALE

ANT

The ant is a tiny but wise creature. The Bible tells us this insect has no leader, but is a very busy worker. The ant collects food during the summer and then stores it for use during the winter.

Ants were common in the Bible times as they are today. The black ant and the brown ant are the most common.

Ants live in groups called colonies, which are made up mostly of worker ants. The worker ants are female ants.

The queen ant lays the eggs and the worker ant takes care of the queen and the baby ant.

The Bible tells us that lazy people can learn a lesson from ants, because ants are hard workers.

Proverbs 6:6–8   *Go to the ant, you sluggard! Consider her ways and be wise, which, having no captain, overseer or ruler, provides her supplies in the summer, and gathers her food in the harvest.*

ASP

The asp is a snake similar to the cobra. The asp, like the cobra, is a poisonous snake. It is found in many parts of the world. This snake lives in a hole in the ground. Its venom (or poison) is fast-acting, and affects the nervous system of its victims. The asp eats small birds and toads.

This snake is a viper, as is the adder. The Bible tells us that wicked people are like the asp, because they lie, and bad things which they say are as bad as the poison of the asp.

Romans 3:13   *Their throat is an open tomb;With their tongues they have practiced deceit;*
The poison of asps is under their lips…

BADGER

The Bible tells us the badger is a wise animal. It is not big, but manages to make a home in the rocks.

The badger has short, strong legs, with toes made for burrowing in the ground. It looks like a weasel, and is nocturnal and hunts at night. The fur of a badger was valuable during Bible times. Its skin was used as an offering to God and was also used to make shoes and sandals.

Badgers eat gophers and other pests, and its face looks like a raccoon's. It is also a shy animal, but can be very powerful and vicious when cornered.

Proverbs 30:26   *The rock badgers are a feeble folk, Yet they make their homes in the crags…*

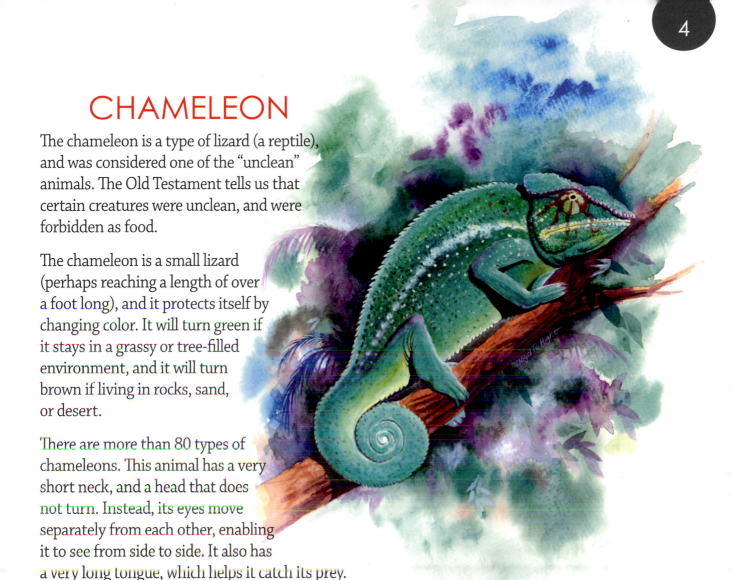

CHAMELEON

The chameleon is a type of lizard (a reptile), and was considered one of the "unclean" animals. The Old Testament tells us that certain creatures were unclean, and were forbidden as food.

The chameleon is a small lizard (perhaps reaching a length of over a foot long), and it protects itself by changing color. It will turn green if it stays in a grassy or tree-filled environment, and it will turn brown if living in rocks, sand, or desert.

There are more than 80 types of chameleons. This animal has a very short neck, and a head that does not turn. Instead, its eyes move separately from each other, enabling it to see from side to side. It also has a very long tongue, which helps it catch its prey.

Leviticus 11:30   *...the gecko, the monitor lizard, the sand reptile, the sand lizard, and the chameleon.*

DEER

There are a number of different types of deer mentioned in the bible. They are: the hart, the hind, the fallow deer, and the roe or roebuck.

In Old Testament times, there was once a wise and wealthy king named Solomon. God was pleased with King Solomon and gave him much wisdom. He had a very large kingdom, and needed many supplies each day for meals. The Bible tells us in 1 Kings 4:22 that King Solomon needed deer and roebuck each day to help provide food for the many people in his kingdom, so we know deer were often hunted in Bible times.

I Kings 4:22–23

Now Solomon's provision for one day was thirty kors of fine flour, sixty kors of meal, ten fatted oxen, twenty oxen from the pastures, and one hundred sheep, besides deer, gazelles, roebucks, and fatted fowl.

DOVE

The dove was the most important bird in Bible times. On the ark, Noah sent out a dove to find the first sign of land after the great waters of the flood had subsided.

Doves are found throughout the world. They are a member of the same group of birds as pigeons, but are smaller. They stay on the ground or in trees, and they eat seeds, fruit, and insects. Doves can fly great distances. They make a cooing sound. They often live in nests and bushes.

Doves were used in Bible times for sacrifice (offering) at the altar. These birds were kept in large numbers in the temples because they were used so often for sacrifice.

The dove is a symbol for the Holy Spirit. It is a gentle bird, and represents the gentleness of Jesus. The Holy Spirit is the comforter that God promised He would send to us for help.

Psalm 55:6

So I said, "Oh, that I had wings like a dove! I would fly away and be at rest…"

EAGLE

From ancient times eagles have been thought of as strong and brave birds. The eagle has sturdy legs and feet, as it has long toes with curved claws, called talons. The eagle is a swift bird. It can fly at very high altitudes, where it builds nests in high places that cannot be easily reached.

In Bible times the eagle was a symbol of great faith, since it's a bird that was so well thought of: strong, brave, and good to its young.

The eagle lives in high rocky mountain areas. It carefully trains and cares for its young. The eagle catches its young on its wings when teaching the babies to fly. This way they are protected from falling from great heights before they can fly easily on their own.

There are a number of places in the Bible which tell about the swiftness (quickness) of the eagle. In the Old Testament, we find the eagle was a bird that was not to be eaten. The bald eagle is pictured on the Great Seal of the United States. For Americans, it is a symbol of strength and courage, just as it was to people in Bible times.

Psalm 103:5

Who satisfies your mouth with good things,
So that your youth is renewed like the eagle's.

FLY

The fly is a two-winged insect. There are about 80,000 different types of flies, and they can be found throughout the world. They like warm places. They have six legs, and can cling to almost any surface. For example, this is why a fly can walk upside-down on the ceiling.

Flies destroy crops, and also carry diseases. In Bible times, God sent swarms of flies onto the people of Egypt, because they would not let Moses and his people (called the Israelites) out of the country.

In the Book of Ecclesiastes, the Bible tells us that dead flies cause a bad odor.

Exodus 8:21

Or else, if you will not let My people go, behold, I will send swarms of flies on you and your servants, on your people and into your houses. The houses of the Egyptians shall be full of swarms of flies, and also the ground on which they stand.

FOX

The fox is the smallest member of the dog family, *canidae*. The fox has thick fur, triangle-shaped ears, and a long, bushy tail. They are fast runners and can reach a speed of 30 miles per hour.

In Bible times, foxes were trouble-some. They caused much damage to vineyards (where grapes were grown). Special watchtowers were built in the vineyards to keep foxes away, because they liked to eat grapes. They also liked to eat animals, birds, and other fruit.

The Bible tells us foxes are found in deserts and live in holes.

Foxes are known to be crafty or sly, meaning they are tricky animals.

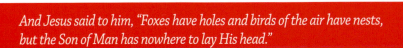

Matthew 8:20   *And Jesus said to him, "Foxes have holes and birds of the air have nests, but the Son of Man has nowhere to lay His head."*

FROG

In Old Testament times, there was a man with the title Pharaoh, who was king of Egypt. He tried to keep the people of Moses in his country, and he would not let them leave. God told Moses to give Pharaoh a message: if he did not let Moses' people go, God would send swarms of frogs onto the land.

The king would not listen to Moses, so God sent millions of frogs into the country. The frogs were everywhere, and even in people's beds. The Bible tells us about this in Psalm 105:30.

Frogs like to be in moist places where there is water. Their body absorbs water through their skin. Some frogs live in trees, but most live near water. Frogs eat insects, worms, and spiders. The frog's tongue is covered with a sticky substance which helps them catch their prey.

Some frogs are edible, which means they can be eaten. People still eat frog legs, and they are served in some restaurants.

Exodus 8:1–2

And the Lord spoke to Moses, "Go to Pharaoh and say to him, 'Thus says the Lord: "Let My people go, that they may serve Me. But if you refuse to let them go, behold, I will smite all your territory with frogs…"

GIER

The gier is a large bird which looks similar to an eagle. It has strong, thick legs, and large wings. When flying, it looks like a falcon. It is also known as the lammergeir (or bearded vulture), the Egyptian vulture, or the ossifrage. In the Book of Leviticus and in the Book of Deuteronomy in the Old Testament it is listed as an unclean bird, and was not to be eaten.

The Egyptian vulture, gier (lammergeir), and the ossifrage are all types of vultures. Vultures help keep down disease by eating dead animals. They locate these dead organisms by using a keen sense of smell.

Deuteronomy 14:17

...the jackdaw, the carrion vulture, the fisher owl..."

GOAT

The goat was an important animal in Bible times. People sold goats for money, ate goat meat, drank goat's milk, and used goats as a sacrifice (offering) to God.

The more goats a man owned, the wealthier he was. Some people owned very large flocks of goats, numbering in the thousands.

Goats were sometimes a larger part of a shepherd's flock than his sheep. The goats were driven ahead of the sheep by the shepherd, and these animals were brought to pastures to eat. When wild, goats live in hilly, rocky country.

Goatskins had a number of uses. Wine bags were made from goatskins, and they were used for stuffing pillows (1 Samuel 19:13). People also made coats and rugs from goatskins. Goat's milk was a favorite drink, and cheese and butter were made from the goat's milk. In Bible times, goats were also given as presents.

Proverbs 27:26 *The lambs will provide your clothing,*
And the goats the price of a field...

HARE

The hare, a member of the rabbit family, is only mentioned twice in the Bible (once in the book of Leviticus and once in the Book of Deuteronomy). The original Hebrew word used by Moses may actually refer to an animal that no longer exists, but the people who translated it into English used "hare" because that is what they thought it meant.

The hare is an unclean animal even though it chews the cud; it does not have a split hoof. Chewing the cud means that an animal chews its food, swallows it and digests it part-way in the stomach. Then the food is returned to the mouth where the animal chews it a second time and then swallows it to be digested the rest of the way in its stomach.

Hares are plentiful in the Bible lands, where there is much desert.

Leviticus 11:6 *...the hare, because it chews the cud but does not have cloven hooves, is unclean to you...*

HAWK

The Bible tells us that the hawk is an unclean animal, and must not be eaten.

The hawk has a strong, curved beak, and powerful claws, called talons. It is carnivorous (meat-eating) and feeds on small rodents, reptiles, and insects. It also has a loud, piercing voice.

The hawk builds its nest on high ledges, or in the tops of trees, safe from predators.

In the Bible the hawk is a symbol of swiftness. It can fly very high and fast, and it also has excellent eyesight.

Job 39:26

*"Does the hawk fly by your wisdom,
And spread its wings toward the south?"*

HERON

In the Old Testament Book of Leviticus, we are told the heron is a bird which is unclean, and was not to be used as food.

The heron is a tall wading bird that looks like a crane, but is smaller. It lives in swampy places and on mud banks. It is a bird that is found all over the world.

One of the best-known herons is called the great blue heron. The bird is three feet long, and when its wings are spread out, they reach almost six feet wide.

There are ten different types of heron in the Bible lands.

Leviticus 11:13–19

...the stork, the heron after its kind, the hoopoe, and the bat.

HORSE

In Bible times, horses were used mostly by kings and warriors in battle. They were also used to pull chariots, which were fancy two-wheeled carts in which kings and other important people would ride.

The horse became a symbol of power in Bible times, and it cost a lot of money to buy a horse, especially if it came with a chariot.

Horses are sure-footed animals, so they were good for battle; however, they could not be ridden in rocky places, because in Bible times there were no horseshoes to protect horses' feet. In battle, horses were protected with armor, and they were prepared and trained for war. Often they were adorned (decorated) with bells on their necks.

The Bible tells us that horses were swifter than eagles, and they were also used for sending messages. King Solomon, a very wealthy king, had 4,000 stalls for horses and chariots.

Isaiah 63:13 *Who led them through the deep, as a horse in the wilderness, That they might not stumble?"*

HYENA

In some Bibles the hyena is called a "wild beast." It is an animal which has the face of a dog, rounded ears like a koala bear, and has a body the shape of a leopard's

The hyena is a predator, which means it eats other animals to survive. It hunts in packs at night, feeding on hoofed animals. It uses its powerful jaws to crush the bones of its prey.

The most well-known is the spotted, or laughing hyena. It is called this because of its cry, which sounds like a person laughing.

Isaiah 13:22 — *The hyenas will howl in their citadels, and jackals in their pleasant palaces. Her time is near to come, and her days will not be prolonged.*

IBEX

The ibex is a type of wild goat. It is a strong animal with a sturdy body and long legs. It lives in high rocky places. It is a brownish-gray color, and has large, curved horns. The ibex is a good jumper that can jump very long distances.

The ibex was hunted so much in the past that now there are laws to protect it from extinction.

Psalm 104:18   *The high hills are for the wild goats;*
The cliffs are a refuge for the rock badgers.

KITE

The kite is a bird with long, slender wings and a long tail that looks similar to a falcon. It is a scavenger, and eats leftover bits of dead animals.

The Bible tells us in the Book of Leviticus, that the kite is a bird that is unclean and not to be eaten. There is another Bible verse in Deuteronomy 14:13, which again tells us this bird is not fit for eating.

The kite builds its nests from twigs high in the trees. Sometimes it nests in trees just above the water. The kite likes warm climates and is found throughout the world. Various kites are found in Bible lands, the most common being the black kite, the red kite, and the yellow-billed kite.

Deuteronomy 14:13

...the red kite, the falcon, and the kite after their kinds...

LAMB

The Bible tells us Jesus is the "Lamb of God."

The lamb is a young sheep. It is protected by the shepherd who cares for it. Just as there were shepherds in Bible times, today we still have shepherds who care for sheep. Shepherds today may dress differently than people in Bible times did, but their job is the same: they tend the sheep, they make sure the sheep are well-fed, safe, and protected from predators.

Jesus is a shepherd to us and His sheep. He is loving and caring, and He watches over us, just as a shepherd watches over his flocks. In the Book of John (John 21:15) in the New Testament, Jesus reminds His disciples to "feed my lambs." By this He meant that they should go and tell God's people everywhere the good news, that Jesus is their Lord and Saviour.

John 21:15

So when they had eaten breakfast, Jesus said to Simon Peter, "Simon, son of Jonah, do you love Me more than these?" He said to Him, "Yes, Lord; You know that I love You." He said to him, "Feed My lambs."

LEOPARD

A leopard is a member of the cat family, *felidae*. It is large, being about four feet long. It is tan-colored and has black spots. Some leopards are completely black; they are called "black panthers."

There were once a lot of leopards living in the Bible lands, but there are fewer today because of the number of people who have hunted them.

The leopard is a good climber, and can even climb trees to hunt its prey.

The Bible tells us the leopard is carnivorous, is fierce, and swift. It lives in mountainous areas, and watches and waits to attack its prey.

Isaiah 11:6 — *The wolf also shall dwell with the lamb, the leopard shall lie down with the young goat, The calf and the young lion and the fatling together; and a little child shall lead them.*

LIZARD

The lizard was common in Bible lands as it is today. It is found all over the world throughout the warmer climates. Lizards have short legs and scaly skin, and most have long tails. Some lizards' tails separate easily from their bodies. This helps a lizard escape from a predator. If a tail is lost, a new one can be easily grown.

In the Old Testament Book of Leviticus, we learn the lizard was an unclean animal, and it was not to be eaten.

Lizards are interesting animals. They can change color to blend in with the area in which they live. If they live in an area with plants and trees, they will probably be green; if they live in the desert, they will most likely be brown.

The lizard also has movable eyelids, their eardrums on the outside of their body.

Leviticus 11:30   *...the gecko, the monitor lizard, the sand reptile, the sand lizard, and the chameleon.*

MOLE

The mole is mentioned in the Bible as an unclean animal in the Book of Leviticus. In Bible times there were no true moles living in those areas, and the word mole most likely refers to the mole rat. People who farm or raise crops do not like moles. They burrow underneath the ground and ruin crops. They have a pointed nose, which helps them dig through the soil. They do not appear to have eyes, as their eyes are covered with skin. They also do not have ears on the outside of their body.

Isaiah 2:20   *In that day a man will cast away his idols of silver and his idols of gold, Which they made, each for himself to worship, to the moles and bats...*

MOUSE

According to Old Testament law (Leviticus 11:29) the mouse is an unclean animal.

Mice live throughout the world. Some live underground, some live on the ground, and some live in trees. They eat seeds, grasses, and fruits.

In Bible times mice were a big problem, especially because mice would destroy much of the grain crop.
Also, homes in Bible times were not tightly sealed as homes are today, and these rodents could easily enter people's homes this way. There was also no garbage pick up in Bible times as there is today, and rubbish piled up along the streets was likely to attract dogs, mice, rats, and other animals. Mice easily spread disease.

The Bible tells us mice were forbidden as food, but there were some Israelites who did eat them.

Isaiah 66:17

*"Those who sanctify themselves and purify themselves, to go to the gardens
After an idol in the midst, eating swine's flesh and the abomination and the mouse,
Shall be consumed together," says the Lord.*

NIGHTHAWK

In the Old Testament (Deuteronomy 14:15) we find that the nighthawk is an unclean bird, and were not to be eaten.

The nighthawk is a long-winged and long-tailed bird, with a large head and large eyes. It gets its name by flying at night in the dark. It feeds on insects, which it catches at night. It is a speckled black, gray, and tan color.

When nighthawks hunt, they often soar high and dive downwards very quickly, swooping in on their prey.

Deuteronomy 14:15

...the ostrich, the short-eared owl, the sea gull, and the hawk after their kinds...

OSPREY

The osprey is a large, fish-eating bird, and is a member of the birds of prey, such as eagles and hawks. In the Old Testament (Leviticus 11:13) the osprey is listed as an unclean bird, not to be eaten.

The osprey lives near the water and feeds on fish. To catch its prey, it glides over the water and swoops down to catch the fish with its powerful talons (claws).

The osprey is dark brown with white on its underside. It builds large nests in trees or in cliffs.

Leviticus 11:13   *And these are they which ye shall have in abomination among the fowls; they shall not be eaten, they are an abomination: the eagle, and the ossifrage, and the ospray…*

OSTRICH

The ostrich is the largest of all birds living today, but it does not fly, even though it has wings and feathers. It can weigh as much as 350 pounds, and is about eight feet tall.

The ostrich is a very quick-running animal. It can reach a speed of about 40 miles per hour. The ostrich likes warm, desert-like climates, which is the climate of the Bible lands.

Ostriches lay their eggs in the sand, but they are easily broken or trampled-on this way. The Bible also tells us the ostrich (Job 39:16) is not a wise bird.

Lamentations 4:3

Even the sea monsters draw out the breast, they give suck to their young ones: the daughter of my people is become cruel, like the ostriches in the wilderness.

OWL

Owls are found all over the world. They have large eyes, but must move their head to see to the left or right. They can turn their head far enough backward to see behind them.

They have soft feathers, large wings, and are a variety of colors: white, brown, tan, and reddish-brown.

Owls are often solitary animals (animals who like to be alone), although burrowing owls and barn owls are frequently found in groups and family bands. They are nocturnal and stay awake to hunt their prey at night. They eat fish, small mammals, insects, and other birds.

The Bible tells us the owl has a sad-sounding voice, is careful of its young, and often lives in deserted cities and houses. It is also an unclean bird, and not to be used as food.

Psalm 102:6   *I am like a pelican of the wilderness: I am like an owl of the desert.*

PALMERWORM

The palmerworm is not really a worm, but instead is the young form of a locust, which looks like a worm. When fully grown, the locust looks like a grasshopper.

The palmerworm is not heard of today, and was most likely a name used in earlier times.

In some versions of the Bible, the word "locust" is used instead of palmerworm.

Amos 4:9

I have smitten you with blasting and mildew: when your gardens and your vineyards and your fig trees and your olive trees increased, the palmerworm devoured them: yet have ye not returned unto me, saith the Lord.

PEACOCK

The peacock is a member of the pheasant family of birds. The male peacock is known for its colorful show of feathers of blue and green. The female peacock – called a peahen – does not have bright colors as the male does.

The peacock has a sharp, high-pitched voice. It eats worms, seeds, insects, and small snakes.

Peacocks were not a native bird to the Bible lands. The Bible tells us they came by cargo ships belonging to King Solomon, who ruled in Bible times.

I Kings 10:22

For the king had at sea a navy of Tharshish with the navy of Hiram: once in three years came the navy of Tharshish, bringing gold, and silver, ivory, and apes, and peacocks.

PELICAN

The pelican is a fish-eating bird and is found in warm climates of the world, and lives near oceans, rivers, and lakes. It feeds on fish. It is a large bird with a very long beak. It has a large pouch-like mouth, which it uses to catch fish. It can store fish in its pouch until it is ready to eat, and its pouch can hold a number of pounds of fish. It also feeds its babies from the fish in its pouch. This bird is also known to gorge itself with fish, and then goes to an isolated place to rest for a few days.

In the Old Testament Book of Leviticus (11:18), the Bible tells us the pelican was unclean and not to be eaten.

Leviticus 11:18   *And the swan, and the pelican, and the gier eagle…*

PYGARG

The pygarg is rarely heard of today, but in Bible times was a wild, bearded goat. It is mentioned in the Old Testament as an animal which could be eaten. In many Bibles the phrase wild goat is used instead of pygarg.

The pygarg lives in desert areas and can go for a long time without water. It has wide hoofs, which enables it to walk over sand without sinking. Today it is nearly extinct.

Deuteronomy 14: 4–5

These are the beasts which ye shall eat: the ox, the sheep, and the goat, The hart, and the roebuck, and the fallow deer, and the wild goat, and the pygarg, and the wild ox, and the chamois.

QUAIL

The quail is a stout bird which looks like a partridge. In Old Testament times God provided Moses and the people of Israel with quail to eat, as they spent many years traveling through the deserts and needed food. The quail was eaten with manna, which was another type of food God provided for the people to eat. It was a dew-like substance God put on the ground, which the people would collect and then eat (Numbers 11:31-32; Psalm 105:40).

Quail feed on insects, grains, and berries. They stay quiet during the day, when they spend time on the ground beneath bushes.
They live in families called coveys.

Proverbs
105:40

The people asked, and he brought quails, and satisfied them with the bread of heaven.

RAM

The ram is a male sheep. It grows strong horns, and in Bible times the horn of a ram was often used as a type of trumpet. Also, skin from these animals was used for the roof of the tabernacle. The tabernacle was a sacred tent that God wanted Moses to build for his people to use for worship.

In the Old Testament there is a story about a man named Abraham. Abraham loved God very much and obeyed Him. God tested Abraham's faith one day. He asked Abraham to offer his own son, Isaac, as a sacrifice. Just as Abraham was ready to take the knife to offer his son to God, an angel of the Lord called out from heaven to tell Abraham to let the boy go. Abraham then saw a ram caught in a thicket. God had provided the ram for Abraham to use as an offering instead of his son. Abraham was thankful, and God was pleased that Abraham was faithful to Him.

Psalm 114:4 *The mountains skipped like rams, and the little hills like lambs.*

SCORPION

The scorpion is found in warm, dry climates. It has a long tail which cures backward over its body when ready to sting. The scorpion stings its prey, and then eats it. It also stings to protect itself. The scorpion's sting is painful and can sometimes cause serious illness or death.

The Bible mentions scorpions a number of times, and they always represent wickedness. Scorpions like warm, dry places, so there were probably many scorpions in the Bible lands. There is a story in the Bible about Jesus gathering a large number of followers. He sent them out by twos to different cities and towns to spread the Word of God. Jesus gave them power over the serpents and scorpions so that they would not be harmed by them.

Scorpions still live in desert lands today. They are nocturnal, and eat spiders and insects.

Luke 10:19   *Behold, I give unto you power to tread on serpents and scorpions, and over all the power of the enemy: and nothing shall by any means hurt you.*

SPARROW

The Bible tells us that God cares even for tiny birds such as sparrows, and that He knows everything that happens to these creatures, even when they fall to the ground.

God tells us we are much more important than sparrows (Matthew 10:29-31). God even knows how many hairs we have on our head.

The sparrow was a common bird in Bible times, and still lives in Bible lands today. It is a small bird with gray/brown feathers. It eats seeds, fruits, and insects on or near the ground, and makes its nest on the ground or in the bushes.

In Bible times, very poor people would give sparrows as an offering to God, since they could not afford sheep or other animals as offerings.

Matthew 10:29–31

Are not two sparrows sold for a farthing? and one of them shall not fall on the ground without your Father. But the very hairs of your head are all numbered. Fear ye not therefore, ye are of more value than many sparrows.

SWALLOW

A swallow is a bird with long, pointed wings. It is a very strong bird in flight, and it is a migrating bird, spending time in the Bible lands part of the year.

From the Bible verse in Psalm 84:3, we know the swallow is a wise, bird, in the way it makes a nest for herself and her young. In Bible times, swallows were known to nest inside the temple.

The swallow feeds on bad bugs such as mosquitoes and gnats. By eating the bad bugs, the swallow helps save crops from being destroyed.

Psalm 84:3   *Yea, the sparrow hath found an house, and the swallow a nest for herself, where she may lay her young, even thine altars, O Lord of hosts, my King, and my God.*

TURTLEDOVE

The turtledove has nothing to do with a turtle, instead it is a type of dove mentioned in the Bible. A dove is a bird that looks much like a pigeon, but is smaller. The dove was often used for sacrifice (offering) to God at the altar during Old Testament times. Poor people who could not afford any other animal for sacrifice would use doves as their offering to God.

In the New Testament (Luke 2:24), the turtledove is spoken of, and was to be offered for sacrifice to God.

The turtle dove is also sometimes called a ringed turtledove. It is a pale, tan color, with a ring of black on the back of its neck.

Luke 2:24

And to offer a sacrifice according to that which is said in the law of the Lord, A pair of turtledoves, or two young pigeons.

TORTOISE

In Old Testament times, the tortoise was common. It was, however, an unclean animal, and was not eaten.

Tortoises live in warm climates. They lay eggs, from which their babies hatch. Some tortoises live as many as 100 years. Tortoises live on land. There are many types of tortoises, and they come in a variety of sizes and shades of green or brown.

Leviticus 11:29 *These also shall be unclean unto you among the creeping things that creep upon the earth; the weasel, and the mouse, and the tortoise after his kind...*

UNICORN

The unicorn is mentioned in some versions of the Bible, but it actually refers to a wild ox. Outside the Bible, the unicorn is a mythical animal, told about in stories, or fairy tales. The unicorn was said to be white, with the head and body of a horse, with one twisting-shaped horn on its head. Bible scholars are not entirely sure of the identity of the biblical unicorn, but it was definitely a real animal. The common interpretation is that this was a wild ox, or possibly a buffalo.

Some wild oxen have one horn, and some have two. The Bible tells us this animal was one of great strength (Job 39:11), and was also difficult to catch.

Job 39:10 *Canst thou bind the unicorn with his band in the furrow? or will he harrow the valleys after thee?*

VIPER

In the Bible, the viper refers to a type of poisonous snake. The head of the viper is wide and triangle-shaped. Its venom (poison) is strong, and affects the blood and tissues of its victim.

There are many types of vipers, and they live mainly in Europe, Africa, and Asia. North and Central America are home to a commonly-feared viper, the rattlesnake. Snakes in the Bible were also known by the names adder and asp.

Jesus had a disciple named Paul. Paul was on a ship which wrecked at sea, and he ended up on an island called Malta. While on the island one day, he was bitten on the hand by a viper. The native people thought Paul would surely die; however, Paul shook the snake off into the fire and was not hurt. Paul was a man who had much faith in God. The native people believed Paul was a very religious man.

Acts 28:3 — *And when Paul had gathered a bundle of sticks, and laid them on the fire, there came a viper out of the heat, and fastened on his hand.*

VULTURE

The vulture is an unclean bird according to the Old Testament in the Bible, and was not eaten.

There are a number of different vultures mentioned in the Bible. The most common vulture in Bible lands is the griffon vulture. Another vulture, the lammergeir or bearded vulture, is the largest vulture. This bird is also known as the ossifrage. This bird will drop dead animals from high places in order to crush its bones. This makes it easier for it to eat these smaller pieces of bones. It has strong throat muscles for eating this type of food. Another vulture is known as the Egyptian vulture, which is the smallest of the vultures.

Vultures live off of dead animals, which is a result of the Fall and the Curse. Before that time, God had provided a perfect world for man. The Bible tells us that vultures have keen eyesight, and that they are always on the watch for prey.

Isaiah 34:15 | *There shall the great owl make her nest, and lay, and hatch, and gather under her shadow: there shall the vultures also be gathered, every one with her mate.*

WEASEL

The weasel is a small, meat-eating animal, and is related to the ferret. It has a long neck, short legs and a snake-like body. It is usually brown with a white underside. It is nocturnal, and feeds on mice, rabbits, rats, snakes, grub, insects, birds, and eggs.

In the Old Testament the weasel was considered an unclean animal, as it was one of the animals that crept upon the earth. The weasel was not a very popular animal in Bible times, and that hasn't changed today! As a matter of fact, weasels are often compared to sneaky people who do things they're not supposed to do. Just as a real weasel will try to steal food, so too, do people sometimes act dishonest.

Leviticus 11:29 — *These also shall be unclean unto you among the creeping things that creep upon the earth; the weasel, and the mouse, and the tortoise after his kind…*

WHALE

There is a story in the Bible about a prophet named Jonah and a whale. One day, God told Jonah to go to a city called Nineveh, which was filled with wicked people. God wanted Jonah to tell the people in Nineveh that God would destroy their city if they did not stop being wicked.

Jonah did not obey God. He was afraid, and he ran away to a place called Joppa, where he sailed in a ship headed to Spain. God sent a strong wind out on the ocean, which was dangerous for Jonah and the other sailors. The sailors were angry when they found out that Jonah had run away from God. "It's your fault we had this terrible storm," the sailors told Jonah, so they threw him into the sea, and a great whale swallowed Jonah. Jonah stayed in the whale's belly for three days and three nights. He was sorry that he had disobeyed God, so God saved him by having the whale spit him out to safety on the shore.

There are other animal names in the Bible which refer to the whale. They are: the sea monster, the dragon, and the great fish.

Matthew 12:40 — *For as Jonas was three days and three nights in the whale's belly; so shall the Son of man be three days and three nights in the heart of the earth.*